THE NEW *CONTENT* *CULTURE*™

THINK LIKE A PUBLISHER TO GROW YOUR BUSINESS

by

Keith R. Reynolds

Edited by Greg Pings

What is your content modus operandi (aka M.O.)?

Introducing the Publisher's M.O.™

The "Publisher's M.O." is a "content hub" marketing strategy and development experience to help brand teams, agencies and entrepreneurs create impactful content and attract new customers.

You will learn to generate return on investment (ROI) with Content Marketing in the age of digital disruption by:

- Demystifying your ROI model

- Developing your strategy

- Getting your team on board

This book has a companion workbook and worksheets available.

ISBN: 978-1-7326652-4-8

ii

"It's not often that such a big idea, not to mention how to successfully implement that idea, can be found in a such a short book. But Keith Reynolds has done it."

Bryan Mattimore,

Author of: *21 Days to a Big Idea*

"Keith's Content Hub strategy is a refreshing perspective for today's business leaders. I especially appreciate the way he organizes the strategies and approaches in his book. Keith's thought leadership is leading the way for content marketing!"

Sandra Long,

Author of: *LinkedIn for Personal Branding: The Ultimate Guide iv*

TABLE OF CONTENTS

vi

ACKNOWLEDGMENTS

According to Scribe, the average book length of the #1 non-fiction bestseller dropped 40% - from 467 pages to 273 pages between 2011 and 2017. My goal while writing was to stay within contemporary attention spans and deliver a book that simply says what it needs to say -- and no more -- to share my experience help you achieve your goals. I could not have done this without the influence of some amazing people:

For Lorna, because every Batman needs a Robin;

For Dan, because justice and a backbone are important;

For Greg, because finding your voice when you're too close to it;

For Lisa, because sometimes we need a little extra content;

For Stan, because inspiration and encouragement...and distribution;

For Bob, because I found my voice;

For Duke, because everybody needs a first break;

For my parents, because roots and wings;

For my kids and step kids, because you help me grow up;

And for Anne, because Aloha.

Beyond inspiration and support from those above, many thanks are due for the direct contributions and editing by Gregory Pings, Lisa Merriam, Cam Magida, Liam Daly and Lorna Bondoc. It has been an inspiring and fulfilling journey—I am so grateful for your help.

Make it a great day.

Keith R. Reynolds

INTRODUCTION

"By 2021, the term 'content marketing' will be defunct as all marketing content rises to high-quality expectations of attention-limited audiences."

-- Magic Quadrant for Content Marketing Platforms, Published 27 March 2018, Gartner

My *aha moment* on the potential of digital content publishing hit me in 1995, when I founded a software start-up. We began producing e-commerce websites and integrating the internet into customer marketing campaigns to fund our dot.com business. I discovered this "new" online channel was directly responsible for 10 to 20 percent of my clients' sales with relatively little effort beyond putting up a website and telling customers. Moreover, marketing these online channels drove more eyeballs to their websites and contributed even more sales. Always with a journalist's eye for storytelling, I have spent my career building digital campaigns for brands and agencies on these following principles, generating tens, if not hundreds of millions of dollars in value for my clients in the process. This book covers everything I have learned about content marketing strategy since before it was called content marketing.

But wait! If Gartner predicted the demise of content marketing by 2021, why are we still talking about this? Here's the point behind Gartner's report: Content marketing will "die" the same way publishing has "died;" which is to say *it won't die at all.*

Of course it won't die! Our various digital devices have become a picture window through which we experience, organize, and interpret our universe. These devices have also become a communications medium for us all to express ourselves to others, to earn a living, and to purchase goods and services with our hard-earned money. We're Hooked!

While technological advances have changed the business model for publishing content, the basic premise of building wealth by publishing content has not changed. And so it is the same case with brand content development:

1. The revolutionary introduction of digital media, mobile and cloud technologies to marketing has changed the type and volume of content we produce;

2. It has changed how your customers consume content; it has changed when they are online, and it has changed where your audience views your content.

3. Most importantly, technology has changed how your company manages the relationships your business depends upon for growth and, set up properly, can support your understanding of whether or not your content is helping you to achieve your business goals.

Number three is critical. We all want to know our Return on Investment (ROI). As one of the pioneers in marketing, John Wanamaker, said long ago:

"Half the money I spend on advertising is wasted; the trouble is I don't know which half"

That statement is no less relevant to marketers today than when made his observation. But today, we have much better tools to measure results.

Despite technological advances, the basics of what makes "good content" has not changed, nor will it ever. We must always engage our audience, our content must prompt understanding, beliefs and action, and these actions must generate value for them and a return on investment for us -- however you define that.

In just a few short years, content marketing technology and social media have truly disrupted the way we go to market, and that is the foundational fact that underpins " The New Content Culture."

Here's YOUR aha **moment:** Think like a publisher to grow your business. Anybody can do it. This book is about why and how to create branded Content Hubs that can grow your business. We'll get more into the definition of a Content Hub, but suffice to say you can think of it like an online magazine.

You'll be amazed at what you can accomplish with a Content Hub-marketing program, and so will your company's higher ups.

With this book, I have distilled my experience into a methodology that will streamline and organize the way you build your Content Hub and provide you with a process to keep it on track. I call it the Publisher's M.O.™ and its value proposition is simple:

- **Demystify** content marketing ROI.

- **Define** your strategy.

- **Implement** with your team.

I know you already have an understanding of what content marketing is; you probably have a team of people cranking out white papers, brochures, videos, podcasts and press releases as you read this. But are you doing it right? Does your content tell your audience what they want, or maybe need, to know for a satisfying experience as opposed to promoting sales messaging disguised as content? Do you publish where they hang out online? Is it in the format they want? Do you have integrated marketing and sales systems in place? Do you measure your success in financial terms? When you update your higher ups on your team's latest return on investment, is the response "wow!" or "meh?"

In other words, are you thinking (and acting) like a publisher? After all, publishers are -- and always have been -- in business to make money, or to achieve some other business goal. Today, brands do not need to look to media companies to create content customers are interested in. Executives want **you** to produce content marketing programs backed by a business case that supports **their** strategy. This book will help you make that case and deliver results.

The Publisher's M.O.™ draws upon more than 20 years of experience of successfully building Content Hubs that generate demand and leads. 30 years, if you count driving customers into analog college bookstores to buy a Personal Computer. You'll learn how marketing with a high-quality Content Hub can fill your sales pipeline and even increase your company's enterprise valuation (what investors think it is worth). With this framework, you'll also find insights on how to define ROI, set a strategy, lay out the roadmap, and get your team on board.

Why a Framework?

Content marketing can become a mishmash of activity with so many elements, tasks, initiatives, and people. With multiple marketing agencies, freelancers, and specializations across a sprawling company – or even a small one, the complexity grows. All that intricacy can make the whole endeavor a bit overwhelming.

A systematic approach ensures that your efforts get you the best results. You will know that your time, energy and resources are being used efficiently. You, your team and your marketing partners will have transparency into goals, activities, status and results. The framework keeps things coordinated, reduces waste, eliminates distractions and prevents missed opportunities. With a repeatable, predictable process that can scale to the size of your opportunity, you can stay agile in a fast-changing, competitive environment.

The Publisher's M.O.™ in The New Content Culture™ today will help you and your team think like a publisher to grow your business. Here's how.

Keith R. Reynolds
Stamford, Connecticut
June, 2019

CHAPTER 1

CONTENT HUB & DEMAND GENERATION 101

I began to formulate strategies based on demand generation techniques I learned while working for IBM at the beginning of my career. This ultimately led me to a realization of the effectiveness of "Content Hubs," though I did not use that terminology at the time. Also described as a portal or online magazine, a Content Hub creates a platform to generate awareness and demand in your market, influence customer decisions, keep your brand top-of-mind with customers and, most importantly, generate and manage leads. The key is to first identify your goals and build a business plan to fill your sales pipeline using media of interest to your customers; then, produce the content it will take to attract customers and move deals along to closure.

My experience at IBM laid the groundwork for my thinking today. In 1987, I began working as IBM's first Collegiate Rep selling PS/2 brand PCs on college campuses. Most students, faculty and staff didn't know how to operate a personal computer, let alone why they might need one. As such, asking college students to sink two to three thousand dollars of hard-earned beer money into what might as well have been a digital typewriter to them was beyond their imaginations.

I wasn't without tools. College bookstores sold a number of DIY books and magazines about personal computers, which allowed my customers to quickly grasp the how-to's of personal computing and understand the technology's potential. IBM also provided me with resources and tools to create awareness and pull people into the bookstore where my team of Collegiate Reps gave demonstrations, answered questions, and handed out materials. We hosted computer fairs, sponsored computer club meetings and so forth. Most importantly, the team collected lead slips that we sent to IBM. Every time a lead matched a sale, the Collegiate Rep who presented the demo earned $25. *Customers actually gave us their names and Social Security numbers in those innocent days!* I rose through the ranks at IBM by pulling data about our marketing programs from various systems and integrating it into a reporting system to help us understand how to improve our efforts. I began this process with simple spreadsheets and eventually used Metaphor DIS software attached to a DB2 database on an IBM 3090 mainframe located some 1,500 miles away in Tampa, FL. By the time we were finished, we had spent $2M and integrated eleven sources of data to produce all the information we needed to run the business unit's $250M end-user marketing campaigns.

My work on the reporting system led me to work for Silicon Valley pioneer, Metaphor, which IBM had just acquired. There, I met a group of visionaries and geeks who were playing with this new "website" technology. I worked on my first website in 1994 that employed a "magazine cover" model (User Interface) to promote the stories inside about musicians and offer downloads of music in MIDI files for them to use. It seems rather quaint now, but it was nothing short of revolutionary back then—and I was hooked!

During my tenure with Metaphor something hit me: The content in those hard copy books on the shelves at the bookstore a few years earlier could just as easily reside on an online network. All a savvy marketer had to do was figure out how to pull customers into a virtual storefront, give them relevant articles, answer their questions and offer them opportunities to take the next step. From today's perspective, this is modern content marketing.

After I left "IBM world" in the mid-90s, I started a digital agency called Maxim Communications and landed my first big account. We created an integrated online marketing campaign for a real estate developer to get people to see his exclusive property in Vermont. The solution was a "Stowe lifestyle" website targeted to affluent people from New York, Boston and Albany. The website was aspirational and had links to cultural and local attractions. We offered coupons for a local B&B. We placed small classified ads with the message, "Live the Stowe Lifestyle," - and our URL - in the vacation home section of the local papers in our target markets. We also placed links from other websites with an affinity to our branded site that offered options to take a next step. The Result: The real estate developer sold his properties and made about $30 million.

New Name, but Tried and True Methods

While the "content marketing" moniker is new, the concept has been around for centuries when it was called *publishing*. People like Ben Franklin, Joseph Pulitzer and William Randolph Hearst each made fortunes in publishing. While many publishers have gone out of business as a result of the technological disruption brought on by the internet, those who understood the evolving technology survived, and continue to thrive today. Moreover, as is always the case with disruptive technology, newcomers, such as Oprah or Arianna Huffington, have secured their fortunes and influence as publishers. Brands like Adobe with CMO.com are in the publishing game today as well. So, we've always lived - and still do - in a culture of content, but it is the evolving technology that puts us in the *New Content Culture™*.

In all cases, these successful publishers did not simply tell great stories. They surrounded their material with a comprehensive program of promotion, events, distribution, feedback and a feedback loop for analysis/reporting. *Think along the lines of reader service cards in printed publications many years ago.*

That's how it will go with content marketing. The ubiquitous nature of high-quality content will force the function: Content marketing will be how effective marketing gets done; therefore, as the Gartner quote from the foreword suggests, the term will simply revert back to - you got it - *marketing*.

A branded Content Hub is a publishing method that concentrates and distributes your digital media and connects to your offline events. It is more than simply pulling traffic to your website. This is a carefully planned "owned media" property that distills your messaging and becomes a force multiplier. Such integrated communications will serve and support your customer's interests. You will create content based on your customer goals as well as the pathways you build for them to achieve them over time. Built on a technology platform, your Content Hub will:

- Bolster audience engagement with news and trends.

- Exchange thought-leading views at an industry or category level.

- Provide your audience with opportunities to watch videos, read articles, sign up for webinars, and catch up on and register for your events.

- Enable downloads of helpful premium content your customers need.

- Earn you authority and trust with search engine algorithms.

With a Content Hub, your customer audience should feel like an honored guest at your "show." The experience aligns your brand with *their values*. One caveat: Be sure your organization is also aligned. Your customer audience will want to talk to human beings in your sales and customer service functions, so make it easy!

A Coordinated Approach

Content marketing is not a series of one-off tactics and initiatives any more than a symphony isn't just a collection of musical notes. The notes are organized and relate to each other. Different instruments contribute voice and mood. The way all of these elements are orchestrated in the overall piece is key to how you feel after you hear the symphony.

That's also how it works with marketing. To mix in another metaphor, consider a Content Hub as a tent where you hold your concert.

The more guide-wires you have in place, the more robust the entire tent becomes for your audience. Your content and events hold the entire structure up. Distribution tactics are the stays or guide-wires that keep the tent pole stable and upright.

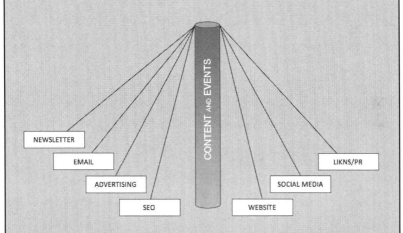

Orchestrating the various content management pieces requires a comprehensive and coordinated framework. Consider all of the pieces not individually, but working together as a system or structure. Integrated information provided by connecting marketing automation and customer relationship management (CRM) systems and processes tie together all the content elements along the customer journey. AND – as a result – you can attribute results to content consumption to measure the outcomes of your content marketing. Now your program has strength and impact-- and you will achieve your goals.

The sky's the limit with how you present your content. A Content Hub serves as a flexible niche-building forum for your business. Give it some personality. WordPress offers themes for a journalistic or magazine "look and feel." Your web designer can certainly also create a custom look. Some companies extend their branded Content Hub to their trade shows and customer events. Others might have several smaller hubs to serve customer segments, leverage keywords, and generate SEO authority.

The Content Hub approach is subtler, but more powerful than hard-sell advertising and more flexible than any individual marketing campaign. The framework can adapt to a small one-person business with limited resources—and yet it can scale to larger multinational enterprises with teams of experts and loads of support. The key is to tie all sources of traffic into your marketing automation and CRM systems and processes. This will create a feedback loop necessary to give you the kind of attribution that is imperative to establish your ROI and the data to evolve your content marketing program with continuous improvement.

CHAPTER 2

WHY A CONTENT HUB?

Today, technology is the reason that publishing content has become a method to promote your business, engage your customers, and deploy your innovative ideas. Brands that offer products and services can base their ROI for content marketing upon engagement, new leads and sales, or channel promotions and research, rather than the former publishing model of selling subscriptions, advertising or sponsorships. The value we now derive is new leads in your sales funnels, data to help us improve our efforts, or keeping a customer another year.

It doesn't matter if you sell books, computers, or trips to outer space. Moreover, the publishing model for success applies beyond products and services. The most successful political candidates use content marketing to great effect, as do recruiters and non-profit fundraisers. Behind every success is a team of savvy market researchers, content creators, social media experts, and marketing automation gurus who know how to identify and connect with their core audience and expand their reach from there to drive desired outcomes.

Social media, search engine optimization (SEO), and content marketing are difficult to explain to executives and investors, because they don't connect directly to the objectives they're measured on, such as revenue growth, profit, market share or brand recognition. As a result of not making this connection, what should be key marketing activities get relegated to the marketing department associates, interns, or to the "techies."

It is no wonder that, according to the Content Marketing Institute/MarketingProfs' *2017 B2B Content Marketing Trends—North America*, "49% of marketing executives say they face Content-Creation Challenges and 49% report that Strategy Issues (lack of strategy, developing/adjusting strategy) impede their success.

This book will help you talk to your executive team or investors about taking a management approach to content marketing, social media, and SEO from their business perspective—and proceed from there to succeed in your efforts by fulfilling their goals and objectives.

Be assured, content is the fuel to achieve management's goals, but you have to be on strategy. Digital marketing and communications impact a business by creating beliefs and incentives that people act upon *and* the systems that they use to become your customer. Perception is everything under this scenario and therein lies the value of content. It is up to you as a publisher to manage the perception and secure resources to get the job done.

The Rocket Metaphor

Consider the "Rocket Metaphor." A rocket is made up of two major systems, the *payload* and the *delivery vehicle.* So, too, is your business.

Your business payload is the experience, products and services you deliver to customers every day. And you are probably damn good at it. Your delivery vehicle is the overall presentation of your business to the various stakeholders you serve. This includes, but is not limited to the business plan, marketing plan, content, sales materials, website, social media, ads, PR, and collateral.

Today, competition is fierce; it comes from new market participants in a very disruptive fashion at a pace never seen before. There is relatively little differentiation between competitive products for potential customers in most markets. Like it or not, your customer offerings, the payload, are therefore largely differentiated by the delivery vehicle.

While most companies often have a myriad of product features that achieve extraordinary results for their customers --core technologies, patented products, problem-solving abilities, consulting services, and training --as you progress from the 'early-adopter' stage on to wide market acceptance, sales are less affected by the offering (payload) than by your overall presentation (delivery vehicle).

Many businesses suffer from a delivery vehicle problem because they see marketing and communications as a cost center. You can often quickly see the correlation when you compare a confusing, poorly maintained or out-of-date website with the other problems a company is experiencing. Often, companies with an overall poor presentation of the business, its products and services will suffer from:

- Low visibility

- Low perceived quality

- Low memorability

- Low sales leads

- Low customer adoption

As a result, you will hear in discussions with executives that the company is experiencing issues with:

- Low market awareness against competition

- Fragmented perception among customers

- Positioning (i.e. "branding") is too strongly influenced by competition

- Early adopters of their innovations are hard to secure

- Competition is based on price in later stage sales

- Sales have plateaued

- There is a lack of working capital

- Equity funding is hard to secure

And then there are the search engines. They have no visibility in areas they should.

Such companies find themselves competing in a world where the customer relationship is created online. Customers are, now more than ever, digital natives. They have access to information and control their own buying process in anonymity. The truly successful brands that you compete against understand this and have, in essence, become media companies in order to meet the customers where they are.

A mentor in the media business once told me, "Perception is reality. Manage it." Similarly, content doesn't just happen. You have to make it happen. That means you need to invest in and cultivate a content culture if you want your rocket to take off.

CHAPTER 3

CONTENT HUB PUBLISHING FUNDAMENTALS

By now, you are probably picking up on the theme that, if you're trying to sell something, or convince people to think differently in some way, your success depends upon the degree that you are able to think -- and act -- like a publisher. You have to build and monetize a loyal audience. Before we go any further, let's agree on a simple definition of publishing:

> "Publishing is the process of production and dissemination of literature, music, or information—the activity of making information available to the general public. In some cases, authors may be their own publishers, meaning originators and developers of content also provide media to deliver and display the content for the same. Also, the word publisher can refer to the individual who leads a publishing company or to a person who owns/heads a magazine or newspaper, though over time as media companies have adapted to a wide range of media.

> Traditionally, the term refers to the distribution of printed works such as books (the "book trade") and newspapers. With the advent of digital information systems and the Internet, the scope of publishing has expanded to include electronic resources such as the electronic versions of books and

periodicals, as well as micropublishing, websites, blogs, video game publishers, and the like."

- <u>Wikipedia</u>

Considering that definition, publishing is a way for brands to deploy a time-tested method across a variety of media to build an audience, achieve commercial success, and create stakeholder value.

You've likely heard the "publishing is dead" mantra. Don't believe it! While it's true that the media and publishing industries have taken it on the chin recently, that doesn't mean publishing is dead. It's not even wounded. The technological innovations that have brought the cost of content creation and distribution to near-zero has upended newspapers and magazines around the world. However, the publishers who served their audience's interests well, embraced new technologies and business models, and adapted to new methods of targeting, distribution and tracking have created opportunities for new market entrants – like you.

Think about it. Humanity has used various forms of technology to communicate for some 40,000 years. Cave paintings gave way to hieroglyphics, which were replaced with alphabets. Technology ramped up with the printing press, followed by the telegraph, radio and television. Each technological leap has sped up communication and improved sensory richness.

Today, the Internet adds computing power that automates functions and augments our intelligence about our communications.

Truly, the most fascinating data point for me about the internet is the speed at which we've adopted the new medium. There is no other market that has grown this fast. In 1995, the Internet had "only" 16 million users.[1] That's a bit more than the population of New England.[2] In 2019, more than four billion people used the internet[3]—more than half the world's population! While this rapid growth has created tremendous opportunity for many, what most don't understand is that you only need to scale your publishing to achieve your goals – Not to the entire internet population. Even though the scale of the internet is unprecedented, and it obscures the fact some of the biggest and best opportunities are the simplest and narrowest of niches. This is why I have chosen the metaphor of the publisher to help you find your audience and navigate your content marketing challenges by connecting with them.

Publishing and media have built wealth for people like Benjamin Franklin, Joseph Pulitzer, William Randolph Hearst, Malcolm Forbes and Ariana Huffington. Each of them used the technology of their time to create value. Technology is the

1   Internet World Stats, "Internet Growth Statistics," https://www.internetworldstats.com/emarketing.htm

2   Wikipedia, "Demographics of New England," https://en.wikipedia.org/wiki/Demographics_of_New_England

3   Internet World Stats, "Internet Growth Statistics," https://www.internetworldstats.com/emarketing.htm

only variable that has changed over the centuries. No doubt, you've heard how the internet democratizes information. This paradigm shift has changed *who* can be a publisher, because media production has been put in the hands of in-house marketing teams and entrepreneurs. This essentially means that every company in the 21st century is an internet-based media company. This foundational fact changes how you take your brand to market.

This is why, in order to make money on the Internet, Chief Marketing Officers, business unit leaders, entrepreneurs and the agencies they work with, must develop a culture of content. Your team must produce and distribute stories that reflect your vision, mission, values and opportunities. Successful companies use a variety of media and technologies to build relationships with their customers. Marketers must define their specific stakeholders and deliver online experiences that serve the audience's needs. Websites, apps, blogs, social media, data, and software programs are all examples of the kinds of information you can publish to win in your core markets.

Focus on Customer Needs, Cares and Annoyances:

Think about why your customer buys, and build your content, events, and activities around helping them succeed. The content you create, the events you attend or produce, and the activities you promote must serve the interests of the customer, not your interest in selling a product.

People buy based on emotion, so justify their decisions with logic and facts. Content marketing builds relationships, and relationships are built on emotion. Savvy sales professionals know that even business purchases are driven by emotions. Things like fear, reassurance, joy, satisfaction, greed, annoyances and pride drive decisions. Promoting a product or service is not content marketing. Instead focus on what the customer needs, wants and cares about in ways that will connect with their intellect and the emotions they live with every day.

The fundamentals of publishing, however, have not changed: Publishers must build an audience, provide thought leadership, and add value for their readers and viewers in an entertaining and informative way to form an experience—and make a profit doing it. A Content Hub is an excellent vehicle to achieve this goal.

Content Hub vs. Website

A Content Hub is a destination that aggregates your demand generation content, such as curated, feature-quality external articles, video, branded thought leadership, user-generated stories, social media and more. Content Hubs are typically smaller than corporate websites, but larger than a blog with various kinds of multimedia content. Like a magazine, your Content Hub should have a name that reflects the value of your offering(s) and connects intellectually and *emotionally* with your ideal buyers.

The key differences between a branded Content Hub and a company website or blog include:

- **Richer experience:** A branded Content Hub uses a media property approach to production.

- **Achieve an outcome:** Your multimedia material should be designed to provide information for your audience that will achieve an outcome in the more sophisticated way that a publisher would.

- **Generate ROI:** Unlike a traditional media outlet, your hub will focus on the value of a new lead for your pipeline, instead of advertising revenues. (Check out this Content Hub ROI calculator.) You might also place a value on customer audience retention.

The media you share on Content Hubs needs to be consumable by both people in your audience and the search engines they frequent. We'll touch on this more, but the fact that you are doing a deep dive on specific topics and generating longer reader/viewership for posts that are helpful and relevant (and thus more likely to get others to link to your Content Hub) is a BIG plus in the "eyes" of search engines.

Ethics and Crafting Your Stories Based on Your Perspective

During a Q&A session of a webinar master class I recently conducted, a participant asked: "Do you ever use 'story jacking' where you relate a current or relevant headline to your brand?" It was a term I was vaguely familiar with, and I related my answer to curating news on your Content Hub as part of your content stack. (The actual term, "news jacking" was coined by David Meerman Scott. The Oxford English Dictionary defines it as the practice of taking advantage of current events or news stories in such a way as to promote or advertise one's product or brand. "Story Jacking," by the way, "is a clever term that might suggest elevating one's own life story or, potentially, 'hijacking' one's thinking to shift internal dialogue," according to a review of Lyssa Danehy deHart's book of the same title. But I digress.)

The key point is, I have since received questions about whether newsjacking is ethical. The clear and definitive answer is: it depends. Does the story or event align with your perspective? Do you offer quality insights? Does your brand have the credibility, or permission from the original storyteller/author, to align with the story? Would Google rank you well for trust and authority on the topic? Will other leaders link to your story? Will people stay on your pages to read what you have to say, or watch your video, because it connects with them? Does linking the news to your brand make sense to your audience, or does it, as advertisers say, create "cognitive dissonance?" In other words, is your brand's conversation on the topic authentic?

Authenticity builds credibility and trust, which are at the core of publishing and journalism. I have written and spoken about brand publishing and trust in the media for several years. In 2017, my good friend, collaborator and fellow brainstormer Jonathan Allen invited me to speak on a panel he moderated called "Media Manipulation and Journalist Integrity" as part of the "Future of Journalism Series." I made the case that today there is a third way in the debate between the polar extremes of advertising and journalism. Fast forward two years and people are writing about the need for brand journalism standards. This is important because brands have a responsibility to produce relevant, interesting *and* accurate information. Remember, the new ROI model for media is predicated on the value of acquiring and keeping customer relationships, at the core of which are accuracy and authenticity.

Success in digital marketing requires you to approach the effort with all the integrity and factual truth of a journalist. In fact, given the stakes for a company, I submit that you have a fiduciary responsibility to adhere to this standard as you assemble information for your customer audience and use literary techniques to express your ideas.

It's okay to have a perspective on the facts, but you must not use alternative facts, as fibbing has been recently called. In fact, customers want your perspective. Ever since Ben Franklin invented the modern media industry, publishers have always offered a perspective. You need only to watch MSNBC and Fox News to see that modern-day journalism includes sharing one's perspective. And, like these media outlets, not everybody will agree with you. But that's okay. Publish anyway.

Why Publishers Act This Way

As Jonathan says, "When you act like a publisher, people treat you like a publisher." Content will add value and retain your online customer audience if it:

- Showcases your expertise

- Empathizes with your customers' joys and pain points

- Provides insights, learning or entertainment

This type of recognition as a thought leader will grant you credibility, build your customer audience, fill your pipeline with leads, and enhance your pricing power in competitive markets. That is the value of storytelling. As prospects get to know your company better, they will feel comfortable telling your sales team *their* story. Soon, they will ask for proposals or add your offering into the shopping cart. You build credibility with editorial prowess and hard work, but you will lose it if your content doesn't have some thought or a methodology behind it.

Publishing is a Business

In bygone days, you had to depend on someone else to be your publisher and you rented that person's audience in the form of advertising. Now, you are your own publisher and you can reach your audience directly. As any publisher would, you still must explain to your boss or your board of directors how your work creates value for the company.

Lose sight of the business goals, and you'll be hard pressed to keep your budget – or your job. An economic model is the key to success for any publishing business, but everyone knows the game has changed over the last 20 years. Instead of advertising, list sales, and sponsorships, today's metric for brands and companies that produce digital media is the value of a customer.

This is why you must think (and act) like a *tech-savvy* publisher, whose audience building efforts feed your demand and lead generation activities. One of the important areas of any business success is an understanding of process. Demand and lead generation are no different. You are trying to string together a series of events and train people in procedures and systems that accomplish the goal, in this case of acquiring new customers. Here are a couple diagrams I have used over the years to illustrate how digital tools support the business process.

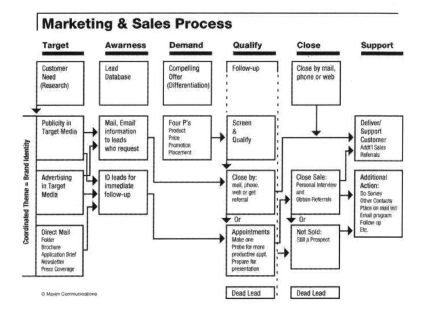

This is a diagram I created around 1996 to explain how the internet could help marketers. Targeting, awareness and each of the demand generation tasks define the essential tasks of building and monetizing an audience. This is exactly what publishers did, and still do. (Note: I did not mention social media simply because it did not exist at the time.)

Online Marketing Process

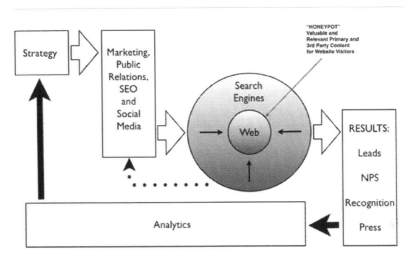

This is a second diagram I created in 2011 to conceptualize for clients how to strategically set up a demand generation system that includes social media and search engines being added to the mix.

Find Your Voice

Being a publisher is not for the timid. Thought leadership is rewarded. In the digital age where anybody can talk about your brand, you must take a "foot forward" approach with your digital presence. As mentioned, not everybody will agree with you, but you will soon learn that you cannot please everybody in a world where your customers and competitors also have a voice. Finding your voice is a must.

Your Content Hub will serve as the virtual window and front door to your business. Google, social media and your public events are the sidewalk. Your content must connect and engage with people who visit your Content Hub. Think of brick and mortar retail stores: their front windows are regularly refreshed with appealing displays in order to make people stop and look. The store window helps customers understand what the store sells, and whether the products match their desires. A well-executed display is rewarded with people who walk in the door.

So it is with Content Hubs. And it is not just people. A technically excellent Content Hub also tells search engines that you're credible, authoritative and trustworthy, which is what SEO and page rankings are all about.

1. People spend more time on a Content Hub than a "Brochureware" website.

2. It is easier to get other high-quality websites to link back to a Content Hub than your "Who We Are; What We Do; Buy My Stuff" website.

These two factors are, in fact, consequential ways that search engines evaluate whether to direct human eyes to your website, read or view your content, and ultimately lead potential customers down your sales funnel.

CHAPTER 4

WHO DOES CONTENT MARKETING?

Even with rapid technological change, you can still take advantage of the tried and true methods to reach your audience. Search engines, for instance, have put the power into your customers' hands by organizing information in a way that satisfies their needs. Knowing this, you can create a content strategy that meets your customers where they're at. And that is why content marketing, and all its derivatives like SEO, have become so important.

That said, the internet is much more than search placement. Social media gives you many ways to plant your brand around in places that reach your audience. Facebook reaches more than one billion people, and email is still highly relevant. But that does not mean you have to reach each of those billions of people. **Instead, focus your activity on the 50, 500, 5,000 or 500,000 people whose problems you're trying to solve.** Get in front of your smaller, targeted audience subset with a spot-on message, and you will more likely reach your ROI numbers.

Three Imperatives: Quality, Authenticity and Alignment

Here's what I know: Prospective customers want your ideas, news, expertise and an emotional connection. They do not want a sales pitch. Your content must establish you, and your company's brand, as "the expert" in their minds. First impressions are everything, and it is up to you to create a positive bias. The customer must believe that the people in your company are advisors and trusted confidants. That is the *why* for "content," and Content Hubs are an effective tool to deliver the goods.

- Here's the secret: Quality trumps quantity when it comes to marketing content and digital media.

- Here's another secret: Production value is vital, but it's not the most important thing; authenticity is.

- And here's the final secret: quality, production value and authenticity will work only if the message is aligned with your customer audience's goals, needs and expectations.

You must first develop a deep understanding of your customers, then offer content that carries relevant information and storytelling techniques. Your content should reflect your organization's cultural values, and connect your online audience to your business. The path to success is paved by effective communication with your customers and stakeholders. But here's a big *IF* – your team must be strategically oriented and trained to use the tools and techniques to grow an audience. This is considered the normal course of business in the publishing industry. You must think like a media mogul and "put on a show" that will interest your customers. This doesn't happen by fiat—you must cultivate a culture of content within your team.

Meet Some Brands That Do Content Marketing Well

Traditional marketers think about their tasks as things that they do – inbound, outbound, attract, close and delight. However, you must think about content as experiences that capture attention, helps people get to know your company, and leads them to believe they should do business with you. In essence, you have to build an audience, provide leadership, engage with people and lead them through the cycle of advocacy. This is what makes the internet such a different medium than any that preceded it.

Indeed, publishing is alive and well in the 21st century. It has always been about growing and monetizing audiences ever since Benjamin Franklin devised the business model for the modern media company. Today, brands can do all the things that publishers do, with one exception: Instead of measuring value in terms of advertisements sold, you express your "profitability" in terms of the value of a new lead, or the value of keeping your customers – that's your return on investment.

Take a look at how these influential brands use publishing fundamentals to capture more business:

Chief Packaging Officer (CPO): www.chiefpackagingofficer.com/ (Esko, formerly Blue Software, formerly Kodak)

"ChiefPackagingOfficer.com presented by Esko | Brand Solutions is a fresh, new information portal for the global packaging community. It's inspired by and dedicated to the talented packaging professionals we've come to know. They are designers, marketers, engineers, innovators, and impeccable managers of highly complex processes, brand advocates, industry experts and – as we call them with great respect, packaging heroes."

This property has survived two M&A transactions because it continually fills the customer funnel with qualified leads and offers a leadership perspective that influences the packaging market. More on this below.

CMO: https://www.cmo.com/ (Adobe)

"Delivers marketing insights, expertise, and inspiration that helps chief marketing officers, senior marketers, and their teams deliver standout experiences in a digital world."

P&G Everyday: https://www.pgeveryday.com/home (Procter and Gamble)

"Helps you embrace real life while providing little ways to make it easier — like recipes, ideas and inspiration for your home, as well as deals on the products you love."

Get Old: https://www.getold.com/ (Pfizer)

"Devoted to the discussion of healthy aging, and the opportunity to increase your life expectancy."

Untapped: https://www.mediusflow.com/Untapped (Medius)

"Untapped is a journalistic portal for financial professionals to stay up to date on Accounts Payable Automation methods, technology trends, news and insight."

Society of Grownups: https://www.societyofgrownups.com/ (Massachusetts Mutual Life Insurance Company)

"Empower you to use your finances to become the kind of grownup you want to be — and even enjoy the journey along the way."

Small Biz Ahead: https://sba.thehartford.com/ (The Hartford)

Insights and advice to help you manage and grow your small business.

IP Radiation Security: https://www.IPRadiationSecurity. com (Keith Reynolds) Leading Digital Convergence of radiation detection and security for a safer world. I built this blog when a startup I founded for got hit hard in the Great Recession of 2008. We had no marketing budget. Within a year of launching it, we were asked to testify to Congress and that led to a referral for a product evaluation by Sandia National Laboratory.

None of these brands, large or small, are traditional publishers. However, they branded their content, named their Content Hubs and built their audiences. This is the future of marketing.

Branded content gives you more relevance to your customer, and, therefore, influence, in addition to added, measurable value for your business. This is not merely pipeline value, this is enterprise value.

I led the agency team that developed *Chief Packaging Officer* for a Kodak division in 2014-2015. This business unit served the packaging industry with workflow automation software that cost $500-$1M. The Content Hub we created offered a full range of information that was relevant to packaging professionals. The basis for our initial effort was curated content, which we combed through and kept only the best five to ten articles per week. We also wrote feature articles about new and innovative trends in packaging. We interviewed packaging executives, published an ROI calculator and sponsored we-binars with industry leaders. We even coaxed an official from the U.S. Food and Drug Administration to participate in a we-binar that helped them get comments from industry on pro-posed regulatory rule changes for food labeling.

The result: We captured 800 leads, of which 57 were sales qualified leads for Kodak. When Kodak sold the division, the acquirer wanted the publication included in the deal. Chief Packaging Officer helped Kodak achieve a valuation for the deal that was eight times over the previous offer they received only two years earlier. Think about it: If your online content publishing generates a deal pipeline and contributes 10-20% (or more) of sales, for a company trading at seven-to-ten times earnings before interest, tax, depreciation and amorti-zation (EBIDTA), that is a lot of value delivered to sharehold-ers. If you don't understand these financial concepts, that is okay, it's sufficient to understand that thought leadership and content create value for owners.

As with any financial transaction, it is possible to model the Content Hub financial contribution using historical pipeline data to make an educated guess about the risks and rewards of investing in a program like those discussed above. When you approach your content strategy and planning like this, you will likely find open ears in your company or with your clients.

The PS: on Chief Packaging Officer is that the acquiring company was bought and the site is still operational as of June 1, 2019 by yet a third company, Esko | Brand Solutions. That is what I would call solid "enterprise value creation" from content.

CHAPTER 5

THE PUBLISHER'S M.O.™

Publishing content is an exercise in leadership, as you may have already gathered. You're on a mission to grow your piece of the business. You are responsible to ensure that your work—and the work of your team—aligns with your customers' needs as well as your organization's overarching objectives. You will think about long-term goals even as short-term realities compete for attention.

The New Content Culture Publisher's M.O.™ is a systematic, objective and agile approach to achieve content marketing, SEO and social media results by producing a Content Hub, as described in Chapter 3. This approach offers a guide for managers, entrepreneurs and agency principals who want to:

1. Create an ROI model that everybody understands—especially the CEO.

2. Define a clear strategy for content marketing, demand generation and sales.

And, with your ROI mwodel and strategy defined, your next step is to supercharge your team, focus their talents, provide a roadmap everyone understands, and set priorities into focused, achievable efforts:

3. **Get your team on board** to transform your goals into traffic, audience and followers for your website or app, as well as generate leads and sales. You will:

- **Create buy-in** and accountability and agree upon goals, milestones and measurable achievements;

- **Coordinate the team's** activity with a proven problem-solving process;

- **Address the challenges** that stand in the way;

- **And embrace the opportunities** that pave the way to success.

- **Time-scale priorities and balance resources** to optimally achieve goals.

- **Communicate and coordinate** to keep stakeholders in the loop.

The Publishers M.O.™ uses a unique 7-plus-7 "bucket" approach to focus your strategy and implementation in order to achieve this level of integration. The seven strategy "buckets" and seven implementation "buckets" step you through the entire process from conception through to assigning roles and responsibilities, setting metrics and utilizing successful meeting protocols. These buckets, or steps are not rigid. Every company is different. They are there for you to build upon and I can assure you that the structure will help you achieve your goals whether you are a startup, or a business unit within a F1000 company. I have used these ideas in all cases.

Seven strategy buckets

Bucket 1 — Northstar Idea: What is the focus of your Content Hub? Your North Star is the central idea that guides your content publishing and media distribution efforts, and connects with your audience. Every great media property, from magazines to TV shows to podcasts, has a North Star Idea that creates an immediate intellectual and emotional connection with the audience – In this case, your customer.

As with all investments, you need to start with some solid market research. What information do your customers look for when they begin their buying process? The market intelligence firm SiriusDecisions has famously reported that 67% of the buyer's journey is digital.[4] Therefore, you must under-

---

4   SiriusPerspectives Blog, "Three Myths of the '67 Percent' Statistic," https://www.siriusdecisions.com/blog/three-myths-of-the-67-percent-statistic

stand what your customers are looking for and the problems they're trying to solve—as articulated *by them*. You know this as the *voice of the customer.*

Now you're able to develop customer personas, a fictionalized description of your best customers. In a B2B context, you must understand if you will deal with CEOs, chief marketing officers, directors, or a marketing associate who is conducting research that will be reported up the organizational chain. Where do they fit demographically? What makes them unique—what are their hobbies, values, or recreations? This is the information your content creators, writers, videographers and graphic designers will assimilate into their work.

Define Your Ideal Customer:

You need to know your audience in order to appeal to them. Take the time to create a marketing persona of your ideal customer. Include users and buyers, which can often be different people. Things to consider for a persona are:

- Age

- Occupation

- Education

- Income level

- Values

- Needs, desires, problems, challenges and frustrations

- Motivations

- Influences

- Media, events, sources of information

Once you have defined your customers, map out how they go about the buying process. How do they become aware of their options? Where do they do their research? How do they shop and buy? After they buy, how do they continue to interact with the brand?

Such experience and understanding of your market is useful, but don't rely 100 % on your gut, because not everyone on your team has your level of knowledge or experience. Surveys and interviews with customers, sales reps and industry leaders, as well as a review of literature from relevant sources will help you round out your answer to the question, "What will I publish on my Content Hub?"

Now you're ready to find a descriptive name for your Content Hub. Think in terms of the name of a publication that connects to the goals, wants and needs of the personas you've identified. It should speak to their emotions and intellect. Here are a couple examples I am familiar with.

Chief Packaging Officer, for instance, is published by Esko, which markets SaaS label and artwork management applications that automate the label and packaging process. The Content Hub seeks to elevate the people who develop packaging for their company's products. Theirs is a strategic function that has multiple touchpoints throughout an organization including legal, marketing and innovation. These managers are responsible for designing and delivering packaging that meet these multiple requirements, including return on investments. The process, according to *CPO's* editorial mission, is complex. As such, the packaging professional's contribution to their company's success should be recognized as deserving a seat at the management table. The editorial team seeks to provide news and information for the packaging community; share ideas and experiences that improve package delivery; and spark conversations around packaging's ability to meet business objectives as well as the packaging professional's evolving role.

Untapped offers insights on accounts payable automation. Published by Medius, a global supplier of invoice automation solutions, this Content Hub highlights the innovative ways an accounts payable function can improve business processes without compromising accuracy or security. This portal keeps finance professionals up to date on AP automation, tech trends, news and insights. *Untapped* targets CFOs, finance vice presidents, accounts payable managers and their teams. Research from Medius' team showed that the accounts payable function is typically viewed as an untapped resource in many organizations. As such, *Untapped's* content shows their readers how to take control of the AP process, improve vendors' performance as well as their process efficiency. With the right tools, people and processes, the AP function can contribute greater value to its business, as well as a higher valuation.

Take a look at the editorial mission statements of the Content Hubs from chapter four, and you will see what they uncovered from their market research.

Bucket 2 — Editorial Strategy: Roll up your sleeves, and define the type of content that will connect with your audience. You must think in terms of topics and themes that actual human individuals are trying to address. While unmet needs in the general market will inform topics and themes, don't make that your exclusive focus. Your strategy will make your content stack take shape: Will you provide tools for your audience, such as ROI calculators for purchasing managers, color selectors, quizzes, surveys or checklists? Which of your topics are best-suited for white papers, feature articles, curated news, infographics, videos or webinars?

Content, Events, and Activities Plan:

Planning the content you will create, and the events and activities you will produce, is critical to your game plan. Determine the key themes you will cover. Chances are, you already have some content that can be used in your program. Audit your materials, existing events and activities. Can they be updated and repurposed? What are the information gaps you can fill? Can you present existing materials in different formats?

Think of themes as pillars of content around which you can expand to support your customer's interests and needs. Generate subtopics across multiple formats to repurpose, expand and enrich the value you provide.

Plan a year of pillar content and events in outline form, then create a detailed three-month timeline that outlines your team's work. Stay three months ahead of yourself. Balance the need for thoroughness and consistency with the need to be agile—you want to jump on new opportunities and respond to change.

Next, match the content types to actual content. Now, your editorial calendar–your content pipeline—is taking shape. It will tell you who will create what, as well as the sources and subject matter experts for the content. Set your deadlines: When are drafts due? How much time for reviews and approvals? When will the content be published? How often will you publish? And make sure that your content is "sticky"— such that people will see the value and stay on your site to read, view or listen to the entire story. The time that your audience spends on your site is a relevant metric for search engine optimization. It's one signal to the Googles, Yahoos and Bings of the world to know that your site is authoritative on a particular topic, and relevant to its audience. It's also an indicator that your audience will start talking to their friends, colleagues and peers about you.

Bucket 3 — Publishing, Promotion, Distribution: Your content is defined and created. Now that you've created the proverbial recipe, it's *time to make the doughnuts* and place your content into the hands of people who will read it, share it and associate it with your brand.

Publish your Content Hub. You want a clean design, intuitive navigation, and descriptions that make sense to your audience. Launch day should include your initial batch of content: articles, videos, infographics and white papers. Give your readers something to chew on, and a reason to come back.

Be sure you also have content for the search engines, such as metatags—keywords or phrases—that tell the search engines what's on your site. You want your publication to be included in search results.

Promote your site within your organization. Employees, especially sales and marketing departments, must know that they should share links and talk up your content. Non-sales/ marketing employees also need to know what you're talking about, and how you talk about it. This will help them tell peers, friends and colleagues what your company does, and even share interesting stories that help explain the concepts. Most important, engage your CMO, CEO and other relevant C-suite leaders in your organization. Their active engagement with your Content Hub tells the rest of the organization, *"This is important."* Remember my point from the foreword, this will be easier if you align your Content Hub's objectives to those that your C-levels' are measured on, such as revenue, market share, or brand recognition.

Promote your content to the external world. Advertise where your target audience hangs out. Send press releases to the media outlets your audience follows. Engage influencers who are respected by your audience. Invite them to contribute bylined material, host webinars, or speak at in-person events. Secure permission from your internal and external influencers to use their photos, quotes and video clips in your content, as well as on social media, press releases, media pitches and advertising. Then there's the easy stuff, like embedded links to your Content Hub in email signatures.

Distribution strategy is a hub-and-spoke model. Your hub, of course, is your Content Hub, and the spokes are activities like social media posts, media pitches, and ads for specific content like white papers or webinars that draw people to your content. Develop relationships with the trade press, and help them secure interviews that feature your senior managers and external influencers. Relationships with editors of sites that report on your topics should result in backlinks on other websites that your audience respects. Backlinks from other content sources like media outlets and partner companies build "authority and trust" among the search engines, as well as your audience. As such, stay away from spam sites or link farms. And finally, the Internet today is a "pay-to-play" game. Gone are the days of free viral marketing. You need to be prepared to buy distribution if you want to scale your content marketing in the niches you play within.

Through it all, keep an eye on traffic metrics. Which pieces perform well? Which ones under-perform? Where did visitors come from? Stay on top of new trends, shifts in your market, emerging technology and networks—stay relevant to your audience, and be sure your content (as well as your distribution tactics) keep up.

Bucket 4 — Community and Events: In many ways, this is a subset of *Bucket 3 distribution,* but it's important enough to be counted as a separate bucket. Community and events are your *in real life* space where you will connect and build relationships with your audience – trade shows, customer events, or community events.

Find all the ways your company promotes itself in the real world, and insert your Content Hub into these events. Share booth space and co-brand with your company, and be sure attendees get a chance to see your Content Hub's name and understand its mission. Give away tchotchkes that pair your Content Hub with your brand, or distribute printed versions of your content with QR codes that take people back to your site.

Trade shows, sponsorships and community events are also sources for stories. What did your company's leaders say at the event? What did the other presenters say? What did attendees want to know, or what do they care about most? Who talked about trends, and what did they say? Did you connect with an influencer who is willing to be interviewed for your publication, or (even better) partner with you on content?

Be sure that your senior executives have bought into your Content Hub and are able to talk about it with attendees or during their speaking engagements. Or perhaps you have identified influencers who follow your publication, and are willing to speak at your company's event or webinar. A great example with CPO, which was previously mentioned, was when we connected with an official from the U.S. Food and Drug Administration who looked up CPO when we asked if they would be a guest on a webinar. The official agreed to talk about proposed changes in food labeling rules, which our team published on CPO. The FDA official was able to discuss proposed changes and get feedback from industry professionals, and *Chief Packaging Officer* was able to offer first-hand perspectives on the rule changes for readers. It was pure thought leadership that helped all parties achieve their objectives.

These tactics work equally well at events sponsored by third parties. Your content that speaks to their event can help them expand their audience, which gives you permission to seek their help to promote your Content Hub and speak to their audience.

I'm telling you, marketing and community events are the gift that keeps on giving.

Bucket 5 — Marketing automation: This is your tech stack: It's how you know when your Content Hub is succeeding or failing. Marketing automation is the key to achieve your return on investment, close your demand-gen loop and keep your goals aligned with your C-level leaders because, done well, it offers an integrated funnel spanning your entire sales funnel.

You have repetitive, cross platform tasks that take a lot of time, and the data they produce is valuable. Your time is better spent analyzing the data and acting upon it, rather than manually collecting and organizing it. This process is ripe for automation, and you'll find no shortage of product or SaaS offerings that can make you more effective.

The key thing to remember is that marketing automation allows you to nurture your audience with valuable content that is pertinent to the person. When you architect your Content Hub to be a closed loop system, marketing automation provides you feedback to move a person down your sales funnel from a prospect to a lead, to a customer and a brand ambassador who recommends you to their peers.

Nielsen Ratings in the media industry are a good way to think of your marketing automation: By designing in a closed loop, or having a control, the numbers will tell you what you're doing right, and compel you to stop doing what doesn't work. After all, you're in business to make money, and you will never make money with content that doesn't invite people in.

Automation improves the conversion and closure stages of the customer acquisition process. But it can be complicated, especially if your company has multiple customer touch points. The best way to "close the loop" is to for your website to be a central hub for all your marketing. All your efforts --email marketing, blogging. search engines, social media, referral links, paid search – should be referred back to your website with a trackable link. Even your offline activity (PR, events, prospect nurturing, sales and customer service) can be encorporated in this. Once someone visits your website, you can cookie them and start tracking their activity. When they trust you with an email address, you can begin to personalize their experience.

As you build your team, be sure to include people who has responsibility for the touch points. Your best bet for this level of integration is to fold your Content Hub into your company's existing marketing automation and CRM package. Develop relationships with those people and get them on board. Their task is to guide potential customers through your company's touch points and help them become (satisfied) customers; the quicker this happens, the sooner you meet (or exceed) your ROI. Marketing automation provides your team the information they need to be successful on their mission.

Successful automation depends on a few more ideas:

- **Constant Care:** Not everything is automated. Yes, the marketing automation tracks engagement, but

someone has to see this and let the content producers know how their piece performed in order to improve. In addition, responses to customer comments
and inquiries must have a human touch, whether it's
a helpful response, or sharing another relevant ar-
ticle—even if it is a "bot." Nothing will defeat your
effort quicker than the dead air that results when a
customer's inquiry is met with silence or an incongru-
ent response.

- **Don't Let Your Guard Down:** Be aware of what your
  brand is saying in various channels. The material you
  publish with marketing automation must be kept up
  to date to support this. Nothing is worse that orphan
  content from old campaigns showing up in search
  engines. If you're not aligned, you'll sow confusion in
  your market. Even if your Content Hub has permission to wander from your company's core sales messages, don't go too far afield. (The folks back home
  are counting on you!)

- **Be Personal:** Marketing automation allows you to
  nurture your audience with valuable content that
  is pertinent to the person based on their expressed
  needs and behavior. You've seen this statement
  before, and I cannot overstate its importance: When
  you move people down your sales pipeline, treat them

like people. "Sir or Madam" or "Dear Valued Customer" is not engaging—you'll likely lose some hard-earned prospects with that kind of tone. Take pains to assure your automated responses sound like a person and be personalized. But automation cannot take you all the way home. Your team must know when it's time to shift responsibility for the responses from a machine to a human who can connect with the person and nurture the relationship. In the end, you want quality, not quantity, in your sales pipeline.

- **Have a Conversation:** Relevance is the difference between spam and automated marketing. You can only be relevant if you understand how your prospect found you, what their interests are and what they need. Think of this as a dialog, not a pitch. Offer value. Listen. Observe. Their behavioral interaction with your content is how you qualify, segment and communicate with your audience, which is your Content Hub's exact *raison d'tere.*

Marketing automation is not your be-all-end-all, and short-term implementation represents a major investment—but it pays off in the long-term. When you understand what automation can do well, and what is done better by humans, you will build your pipeline, and you will be able to demonstrate to your board, your boss or your client how well you hit their ROI target.

Bucket 6 — Sales Model: Without this connection, then why are you producing content at all? If you're trying to fill the sales pipeline, then you must engage your organization's field sales team for insights on content, and preferred delivery channels. The sales team is a partner who will co-nurture your audience. Together, you are trying to optimize the process of capturing leads, tracking their activities and behavior, qualifying them, giving them constant attention to make them sales-ready -- and then passing them on to the sales team so they can be efficient with their time by focusing on the most qualified leads.

The sales process your business follows will help you determine which CRM tool you will use, and how you will set it up. Are you funneling leads to an online shopping cart? Are you a B2B player that touches multiple decision makers? Or is this a hybrid where people order online and have an account executive? Your content must support the process, and it must address each target as an individual buyer, even when your selling to a large, matrixed enterprise. Your content must be on strategy, and it must align with the sales team's messaging platform and strategy. You cannot afford confusion, because your sales team owns the customer relationship.

Your data should enable sales. Data about your customer's behavior at various points in the sales cycle allows you to optimize your messages and delivery methods so that the sales team can convert leads and close deals. Technology tools like HubSpot with the support of your IT team or integration partners can help you:

1. **Create** actionable sales pipelines and more accurate sales forecasting;

2. **Translate** insights into the content and activities that contribute the highest ROI;

3. **And shorten** sales cycles by aligning your marketing and sales functions.

Connecting Content to Your Business

Content and event marketing is not selling, but it most definitely supports sales and business development. Map your content and events to your business. This is a critical first step in content marketing.

For sales, use a lead capture process to connect you with the people who find and engage with your content, then follow up with them. Involve your sales team, communicate with them. Your sales team must know what is in your content plan, and how to use it in order to start and deepen relationships with their prospects and customers. When people request a copy of your white papers, who calls them? What about the people who like, share or comment on a social media post? Someone must follow up with them as well.

Keep in mind the "golden hour" rule: The chance of a passing interest converting into a real lead is highest within the first 60 minutes of the initial interaction. If you wait a day to respond, you have lost most of the value of the potential interest. The more integrated your systems, the easier this level of follow-up will be.

Success does not come with the sales team alone. Look beyond sales to other places where your content can make a difference. Customer service, billing and accounting, partnership development, and innovation are areas where content can contribute to better, more productive and profitable customer relationships.

When your sales reps or distribution partners look at your Content Hub, they have to understand how this will help them hit their targets. Your best selling point to these professionals is the opportunity to upgrade themselves from order-takers to trusted advisors. Help them understand your editorial framework so they can use your material in their sales calls, and incorporate thought leadership into their customer conversations. Sales reps understand their customers' pain points; you have to make it easy for them to find relevant articles in your content library that can help them answer questions and advance conversations.

Salespeople are paid to identify their customers' budgets and buying times. Customers, on the other hand, are trying to solve problems and get things done. As such, sales people must know what their customers are reading so they can tailor their conversations. All of a sudden, your sales reps are having advisory conversations about a solution, and the customer is moving down the pipeline. That's an actionable lead. That takes training to make happen.

It is important that you also train salespeople to handle inbound leads. They are different than a lead met at a trade show, or on a cold prospecting call. The likelihood is that a person who has downloaded a content asset will not want to engage in chit-chat or start talking about their budget. They have taken the time to educate themselves and collect information. Start with what it is they are looking to do.

Because your sales team is on the frontlines of customer relationships, they very often have some of the best ideas for bottom of the funnel content that can be translated from a sales conversation to a valuable media experience. Items like ROI calculators, color selectors and configurators, as well as "readiness checklists" can often be sourced from your sales team because they spend a lot of time qualifying your customers.

Bucket 7 — ROI model: Return on investment. This is how you know whether your outcomes are profitable or if you're achieving what you set out to do. Your ROI will tell you if you're producing content that makes sense to your audience. What is your goal? Collecting email addresses? Selling products and services? Gaining influence in the market? Recruiting employees? Conducting market research? Everything you do must center around the value you place on a lead and the outcomes. The more concrete the measurement, the easier it is to track success. Just keep in mind educator Steve Hargadon's observation that, "Not everything worthwhile can be measured, and not everything that can be measured is worthwhile."

Measuring Content Hub Results

Prove the value of your work, and the effectiveness of your strategy by measuring and analyzing your results. The metrics you use will depend on the goals you set— and on your ability to capture data. The list below is not exhaustive, but it is a starting point.

Sales metrics

- Leads captured

- How many leads are marketing qualified (MQL) and sales qualified (SQL)

- Conversion rate

- Cost of customer acquisition

- Customer retention

- Incremental sales growth

Digital marketing metrics

- Number of visitors, new and returning

- Time on site

- Number of pages visited

- Bounce rate

- Sources of traffic

- Pages visited

- Click through rate

- Response rate

- Downloads

- Form completions, sign ups

- Cost per action

- Your site's domain authority

- Followers, subscribers

- Comments, shares

- Cost per click

- Social sentiment

- Email opens, forwards, clicks

General marketing metrics

- Brand awareness

- Customer engagement

- Marketing spend per customer

- Return on marketing investment

- Lifetime value of a customer (LTV)

- Share of market

- Net Promoter Score (NPS**)**

A Practical ROI Model

Your ROI model should include not only what you are creating, but how you will distribute and promote the content and events, and how you will foster audience engagement. Your plan should specify needed resources, staffing requirements, interdependencies and timing. I have published a simple Content Marketing <u>ROI Calculator</u> to help you. Among the inputs:

- **Program costs:** Salaries, fees, freelancers, designers as well as the costs for advertising content and events, CRM and marketing automation software— everything you spent to build your Content Hub and keep it running year-round.

- **Average sale:** The value of products or consumables.

- **Length of contract:** The length of time for service on product installations, a license agreement on software, or a service such as consulting, freelancing, or ongoing maintenance is to be delivered.

  - **Additional revenue:** Think the "blades" from the razor and blades analogy. How can you develop an ongoing relationship with your customers?

- **Number of visitors:** How many people do you expect will visit your Content Hub?

- **Number of conversions, opportunities and sales:** How many visitors will actually decide to buy your product or service?

My ROI calculator includes an E:R metric—that's expense divided by the revenue – you can generate. It varies by industry and company, but any number below .33 generally means your project is "a go," and will show how your publishing model is an investment, not an expense. For every dollar you invest, you get three dollars in return. It's how you will show your CEO, CFO, CMO, and others in your C-suite, how your Content Hub aligns with their goals, which typically revolve around revenue and profit.

A credible ROI model will help you make the case for the investment, and—once your sales start to roll in—will validate your program's effectiveness and set the stage for optimization.

A good ROI model gets respect and attention from the board room and C-suite execs. It will also help you understand how your content contributes to customer acquisition as well as customer retention. Now, you're able to understand how your messaging impacts your company's valuation. (It should increase!) Best of all, this will help you make your case for any marketing program, be it content marketing or showing students your latest gadgets in a Daytona Beach beer tent during spring break.

If your company or business unit is undergoing negotiations for sale to another company, the size of your pipeline and your ROI model will likely become a factor in the M&A negotiations. The numbers don't lie: This is more than full pipelines or bars on a chart, your ROI puts an actual value on the revenue it brings in.

So back to the value of a lead: Is your value based on how much revenue you generate? Is it the lifetime value of a lead that becomes revenue? Or is it the value of your influence in the marketplace, or perhaps the comments and Net Promoter Scores (NPS) of site visitors? Each of these are valid outcomes. What are you trying to achieve?

Seven Implementation Buckets

Today, we work in flatter, more networked and geographically dispersed teams. Pulling off your content strategy requires a cross-functional and almost always a cross organizational approach. Here are seven buckets for you to use in your efforts to get your team on board and working together with accountability to each other to get things accomplished.

Bucket 1 — *Team and Roles:* Who does what, and who's in charge? Agency personnel, freelancers, video producers, graphic designers, SEO consultants, web gurus, marketing strategists, sales leaders, or others? Not everyone reports to the managing editor, so you must achieve buy-in from the leaders of various functions in your organization. Everyone must see themselves as a vital, contributing part of your team. They will help you succeed, so you must develop these relationships.

Bucket 2 — Customers: Understand who they are. In a B2B scenario, you must understand whether you're talking to the C-suite, a purchasing manager, a medical coder, or a middle manager who wants to make smart recommendations to a management committee. Whoever it is, you must know their needs, their journey, their goals, hobbies and habits. In brief, what kind of content will they read, watch, take note of and share? Developing a set of personas that are a fictionalized representation of your best customer types is an invaluable exercise to get your content team up to speed.

Bucket 3 — Vision: Create a clear picture of the destination that reveals your brand leadership. For instance, *Chief Packaging Officer* understood the packaging professional's status in the organization, as well as that person's conviction that they produce significant–if unnoticed–value to the organization.

The vision was to produce a significant voice in the industry and become a clearinghouse of thought leadership.

Bucket 4 — Roadmap: Your mission, purpose and values that describe your team, and enable them to achieve your goals.

- **Long Term Goals: 10 & 3 Years** – It helps to get everybody on the team thinking about your BHAG (Big, Hairy, Audacious Goal, pronounced "BEE- hag" from the book Built to Last by Jim Collins). What does your company and publishing effort look like in ten years? What would it look like in 3-5 years if you are going to achieve your ten-year vision?

- **Market Assessment:** What's the market like–is it fragmented, monopolistic or regulated? What forces are at play? What does the media covering the market look like? After all, you will compete against them—and align with them as well.

- **Competition:** A SWOT analysis–identifying your **S**trengths, **W**eaknesses, **O**pportunities and **T**hreats– will help you understand the internal and external factors that will help or hinder your progress.

- **Go-to-Market:** These materials include your elevator pitch, target market, three differentiators, proven methodology and your promise to your audience.

- **Sales Enablement:** Identify the content that will support the sales process, and efforts to teach your sales team how to use your published material to achieve their goals.

- **Stakeholder Experience Builder:** What are the things your team must do on a periodic basis to give your stakeholders a great experience? How can you automate this? Who is responsible?

You cannot expect a team of people to produce content that adequately represents your company without this information. If your company already has this available for your content producers, make sure to organize it in a centralized fashion to share with your content team. If not, take this as an opportunity to get the work done.

Bucket 5 — Goals, Milestones and Metrics: S.M.A.R.T. objectives — Specific, Measurable, Achievable, Realistic and Time-bound. Your team needs concrete and realistic action items. Write them down and keep them in front of everyone. Goals are achievable in six-months to a year. Milestones can be accomplished within a quarter or two, max. To-do's must be completed within two weeks, or a month at the longest. Each priority item must be categorized by time-scale and assigned to a person on your team, who must be accountable for getting the item done. The goal of your meetings is to move these items into the "graveyard" because that means you are getting stuff done (GSD) and moving the ball forward.

Bucket 6 — Red and Green Flags: Red flags are problems that stand in the way of success. Identify them. Discuss them. Assign them to someone, and hold that person responsible. Green flags are opportunities that pave the way to success. Assign them to someone, and hold that person responsible. Write them down and keep them in your weekly agenda. Prioritize all of these for discussion by evaluating the quadrant below:

Prioritizing Red and Green Flags

VALUE DERIVED		
High	**Medium**
Medium	**Low**

Resources Needed to Address Flag (People, Time & Money)

With your list of problems and opportunities prioritized, select the one you think needs work the most and follow-this routing for handling your flags.

1. Prioritize Flags

2. Select One

3. Define Root Cause (Five Why's + Data)

4. Openly Explore Alternatives

5. Agree on Next Steps and then

6. Resolve:

    A. Close Out as done or

    B. Move to the To-do, Milestones or Goals List.

Bucket 7 — Meeting Protocols: Effective communication forges high levels of accountability, commitment and performance, whether you're working with in-house or virtual content teams; or a hybrid. Every meeting has an agenda; each agenda item has a time limit. Assign a timekeeper who will remind everyone when it's time to wrap up a discussion and move on to the next item. Assign someone else to keep the conversations on track, and identify topics that should be discussed offline if need be. Most importantly, every member must be comfortable enforcing good meeting hygiene, such as muting your line on teleconferences when you're not talking, or stopping the cross-talk during in-person team meetings.

Here is a recommended meeting agenda to insure your team stays on track:

Lead-in - Prompt: "Something excellent personally & professionally that happened last week."	**3 Min**
Team News / External News	**2 Min.**
Key Metrics	**5 Min**
Goals & Milestones	**5 Min**
To-Do List	**5 Min**
Red & Green Flags	**35-65 Min**

- Root Cause Analysis (5 Whys + Data)
- Open Discussion
- Close as a To-do, Milestone or Goal

Conclude	**5 Min**

- Recap To Do's & Milestones
- Identify Takeaways
- Bullhorn
- How Did We Do?

Having a methodology to guide your content publishing activity and get your team in line with the strategic imperatives of your business will help to ensure your success.

CHAPTER 6

PULL OFF YOUR STRATEGY

Malcolm Forbes has a gift for stating what ought to be obvious, but usually is not. "If you don't know what you want to do," he once observed, "it's harder to do it."

Setting Goals for Your Content:

Setting specific goals is a first step in building out your business growth framework. Typical goals may be targeted to:

- Brand, such as increasing awareness and understanding of your business, products and services, features or culture.

- Sales, like feeding the top of the sales funnel and opening relationships, on down to nurturing leads.

- Post-sale, such as deepening relationships through up-selling, cross-selling, reordering and referrals.

Make your goals specific and measurable. Tie your content marketing goals to overall business goals and objectives, and coordinate buy-in with senior managers and across company functions.

Marketing is no longer the job of the marketing department alone. Your goal-setting exercise must include senior managers, department leaders and public-facing staff across your company's functions. Equally important, include timing in your goals, starting with short-term (approximately three months), as well as long term (a year or more.)

Content is king, and your audience is the queen. The bigger your customer audience, the higher the probability some of them will become leads—and your sales team will write proposals.

The key to content marketing success, as we've seen, is to build a Content Hub and use digital technology to integrate your sales and marketing into a single funnel. Marketing automation and CRM (whether spreadsheets, Zoho, Infusionsoft, Hubspot, Marketo, Act-On, Eloqua, or one of the hundreds of other marketing automation solutions) will help you scale these conversations and manage deals with prospects in an orderly manner. And then get your human capital organized for success with an agile-like standing meeting agenda to become a high performance team.

Content Model to Enhance Influence and Revenue Impact

<u>Lisa Merriem</u>, a colleague and leading branding and content marketing expert, notes that effective orchestration of content, events and other activities can be expressed in a simple equation:

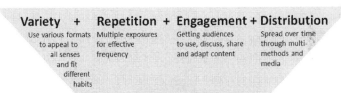

Variety +   Repetition + Engagement + Distribution

Use various formats to appeal to all senses and fit different habits

Multiple exposures for effective frequency

Getting audiences to use, discuss, share and adapt content

Spread over time through multi- methods and media

= Influential Impact

Variety is the first variable. Express each idea you have for content in more than one format. It is better to have fewer ideas with greater variety of expression. People absorb information better when they encounter it in different ways. Developing ideas is expensive: Expressing them in many ways wrings the greatest value out of each idea.

Take the example of a webinar. You and your team will likely spend significant time, brainpower and energy producing and promoting it. Once you have your webinar content, you can easily expand it to other formats. Your webinar can be expressed in the following ways:

- Transcript

- Summary sheet of highlights

- Series of pull-quotes

- Blog articles

- Bylined magazine articles

- Set of infographics

- Video and audio podcast, whole or in parts

- Online Q&A and discussion

- Newsletter content

- Checklist

- Package of tools, worksheets, templates, calculators

The content from your webinar can be further repurposed for:

- Media appearances

- Workshops

- Conferences

- Keynotes

- Roundtables

- Case studies/real world stories

- Original research/review existing research

- White papers

- Books

- Brochures

- Training courses

- Animations

- Interviews

- Guest blogs

- Quotes

- Testimonials

- News releases, announcements

- Comparisons

- Glossary

- Mobile apps

- How-to and how-not-to

- Challenges

- Opinions and debates

- Predictions

- "Fail" Stories

- Demonstrations

- Awards

- Polls/surveys/quizzes

- Sponsorships

- Resource library

Repetition is related to variety. The more often you repeat and reprise your content, the more likely it will be seen, remembered, understood and valued. Thomas Smith, an early advertising thought leader, summed up the process in his book *Successful Advertising* published in 1885.

The 1st time people look at the ad, they don't see it.

The 2nd time, they don't notice it.

The 3rd time, they are aware that it is there.

The 4th time, they have a fleeting sense that they've seen it before.

The 5th time, they actually read the ad.

The 6th time, they thumb their nose at it.

The 7th time, they get a little irritated with it.

The 8th time, they think, "Here's that confounded ad again."

The 9th time, they wonder if they're missing out on something.

The 10th time, they ask their friends or neighbors if they've tried it.

The 11th time, they wonder how the company is paying for all these ads.

The 12th time, they start to think that it must be a good product.

The 13th time, they feel the product has value.

The 14th time, they believe they've wanted a product like this for a long time.

The 15th time, they yearn for it because they can't afford to buy it.

The 16th time, they realize that they will buy it sometime in the future.

The 17th time, they make a commitment to buy the product.

Engagement is the motivating force of content marketing. What do you want people to do in response to your content? You must define the "what next" of your audience's reaction, then create content campaigns, events and activities toward that purpose. Use this list to specify one or several specific responses:

Read it

See it and watch it

Hear it

Comment on it

Share it

Debate it

Adapt it

Use it

Buy it

Buy more

Recommend it

Distribution is how your work gets in front of the people who matter. No matter how excellent your content is, you will not achieve your goals if your audience doesn't see it. Use multiple distribution techniques to reach the greatest audience multiple times.

SEO is the place to start. SEO, the art of making your content findable, has been around for decades. However, many marketers still do not understand the basics of search, or formally create an SEO strategy. Content without search is like a car with no wheels or gasoline. Whether your content is online, or you are producing live events, people use search engines to find you. If it exists anywhere, people expect to find it online. The good news is that solid SEO strategy is also a roadmap for solid content from an audience perspective.

Other typical distribution methods to get people to see and engage with your content include:

- Email promotion

- Regular physical mail

- Organic Search (SEO)

- Paid search such as AdWords (SEM)

- Content placement, such as Wikipedia, SlideShare, Quora, Scribd

- Association pages, lists, community pages/forums, media, events

- Paid display ads and promotions (traditional and digital)

- Out of home advertising

- In-store

- At trade shows

- Embedded links

- Topic and newsjacking

- RSS, sharing on Reddit, Digg, StumbleUpon

- Cost per click placements

- Internal links

- Social posting, group engagement, paid ads, social buttons

- Influencer marketing: Who in your network can influence your audience?

While some distribution methods are free, the old adage "you get what you pay for" still applies. It's possible your idea may organically take off, spreading like wildfire at no cost, however such a phenomenon is exceedingly rare. You can post an idea on social media, but almost no one will see the post unless you pay to boost it to a targeted audience.

The competition for attention about your webinar is keen. People are bombarded with more messages than they can possibly consume. A solid strategy taking into account the variety of content, need for repetition, means of engagement and types of distribution backed by a generous promotional budget is the only way to break through, though the impact in terms of market influence and revenue impact can be huge if you have a solid approach.

You can see how many internal people, freelancers, agencies and internal departments a program like this involves. But you can also see how such an effort to build out content from a webinar can have incredible ROI if managed well.

Wrap-up

"The New Content Culture"™ is a concept that encompasses all of the big lessons I've learned in demand gen marketing and put them in a contemporary context. During a recent Q&A session where I had presented the Publisher's M.O.™, someone asked me why I call it the "new" content culture. Maybe he was trying to be a wise guy, but his was an excellent question. He's right, of course—none of these concepts are new. But the technology is new. As such, we are all surrounded by large amounts of content that would have been unthinkable just 10 or 20 years ago. When technological breakthroughs make something faster, cheaper, and put capabilities into more people's hands, we often assume that the common-sense rules and habits that our parents followed no longer matter. Well, they do matter. Why? While technology has changed, people have not.

The Publisher's M.O.™ is simply a means, or methodology, outlining how you know what you want to do and how to go about doing it. Each of the strategy and implementation buckets may seem obvious, but so very often are ignored or skipped in the rush to get things done. That's why some publishers fail; it's why marketing managers scratch their heads and wonder why no one is getting the message, or why results are lagging.

We have always filtered the information the world throws at us. We still need to be convinced that one message should have precedence over another. We still need to make a business case to justify the use of resources versus an alternative strategy we might pursue. And we don't want to waste our time, or the time of our stakeholders. If anything, technology has amplified these human imperatives. That's why you must produce content that tells people what they need to know, and your content must fill a need–yours and your audience's. When we re-learn these age-old truths about being relevant *in the eyes of our customer audience,* the knowledge becomes new. Again.

The Publisher's M.O.™ is not a monolithic program that you must implement in a specific way. Some managers and teams are more process oriented than others. Take an approach of constant adaptation and evolution that supports changes in your organization, the market, general trends and new best practices. Keep your eyes open to learning opportunities to keep refining your program.

I'll close with eight truths that developing the Publisher's M.O.™ has taught me – they're basically everything in this book packaged into 140 words:

1. Publishers are in business to grow and monetize an audience. So are you.

2. Start by asking, "Who is your audience and what are you trying to accomplish?" Put a value on that.

3. Provide the information your customers want and need. Make "the show" about them, not about you.

4. Your Content Hub is a startup. Be agile. Think in terms of "Most Viable Product." Simplify. Start with what you can muster and grow.

5. Engineer your demand generation process using "user experience" and "design-thinking" methods.

6. Scale your branded SEO content with customer audience data and insights by sharing them among the team.

7.   Culture counts. Empower your team with a rich, supportive culture that encourages debate.

8.   Model your team members' accountability by providing them with the resources they need, a clearly identified strategy and program management, and a voice in the debate. You'll be surprised what can be accomplished.

I won't wish you luck, because luck has little to do with success in publishing and marketing. Success is built on strategy, culture and teamwork and having a system that produces relevant content on a consistent basis. But I do wish you good fortune, because you will surely find it when you, "think a publisher."

Last Thoughts

Thanks for reading my book. I would be honored to hear how your own publisher's journey progresses. Please let me know if you would like me to run a workshop or if you would like to use my workbook to put your own content marketing strategy together.

Made in the USA
Columbia, SC
18 September 2019